THE WIDOWS MIGHT

THE WIDOWS MIGHT

By Apostle Darlyn C. Turner

Published by CedarLife Publishing

Unless otherwise noted, all scripture quotations are from the King James Version of the bible.

Cover designed by Jose Pepito Jr.

ISBN: 978-1-7335241-4-8

DEDICATION

This book must be dedicated to one of the greatest men to ever walk this earth, my husband, Dr. Clifford E. Turner. I cannot express in words what he meant to me, what he gave me, and what he left for me. Even in death, because of his insight, foresight, and vision, many are still receiving the new, the next and the now from his words of wisdom, prophecies, books, sermons, and innumerable memories that are forever in our hearts. He would often announce that when he died, I could live off the memories. One thing is for sure, his memory is still bringing life to the masses. I will love you forever, and I am forever grateful that God chose me to be by your side for the last 21 years of your life.

Table of Contents

ACKNOWLEDGMENTS

I must acknowledge the over 258 million widows worldwide whose lives have been interrupted with sudden singleness without their consent, approval, or preparation. May you connect with God's ultimate purpose for your life, and may you forever walk in the promises, protection, and authority that belongs to you in this season.

INTRODUCTION

Widowhood is a realm unlike any other. A widow's world changes on every level, mentally, emotionally, socially, financially and spiritually. Being "single" after widowhood differs from being single in any other fashion.

Firstly, being single (as in never married) is like being a virgin. Once it is gone, you never truly can return to it because you will always carry your experience in your soul. Singleness is sacred, treat it as such… and carefully consider who you will "carry" for the rest of your life.

After divorce or widowhood, singleness is unique, as the ripping apart of your heart, mind, emotions, property and sometimes even your identity take place. This type of singleness creates another aspect of your existence, therefore negating any idea of "singleness" as the layers of your soul and experiences have been altered forever. Your life as you have known it and even imagined has now been destroyed and the rebuilding process must begin again. God has made it clear in His word His concern for the widow.

Psalm 68:5 says, "A father of the fatherless and a judge for the widows, is God in his holy habitation." Deuteronomy 10:18 says, "he executes justice for the orphan and the widow..." In Malachi 3:5 God says, "I will be quick to testify against those who oppress the widows..."

So, God says He is the judge, jury, and witness for the widow!

GOD COMMANDS FOR THE WIDOWS TO BE HONORED, AND NOT OPPRESSED.

So, why are 50% of widows in poverty? How is it that even those who name the name of our Lord Jesus, seem to ignore the plight of the widows? You will be hard-pressed to find a widow ministry in the average church. Many former wives of pastors and leaders are quickly thrown out, discarded, and mistreated upon the death of their spouse. How can this be among the redeemed? Practically every scripture that speaks about the poor, speaks about the widow.

Isaiah 1:17 commands us to plead for the widow. This is the responsibility of every believer, particularly to attend to those who are "widows indeed" according to 1 Timothy 5:3. However, this book intends to stir up the voices and the authority of the widow, a strength that only comes through the conduit of death. John 12:24 says, "...except a corn of wheat fall into the ground and die, it abideth alone." Just like our salvation, there is a life (Zoe) that is created from death that, "bringeth forth much fruit."

We see throughout scripture, particularly in the new testament, that the widow was commended for her faithfulness (Luke 2:36-38), her giving (Luke 21:1-4), and her tenacity (Luke 18:1-8). There is perseverance, a proper perspective on life, things, and an attitude of "nothing else to lose" that can empower a widow that decides to walk in her God-ordained season. I believe this power helped to fuel Anna's relentless faithfulness to the house of God and prayer, the poor widows' willingness to give out of her poverty, and the widow needing justice refusing to relent before the judge.

Much like the widow that pleaded her case before the unrighteous judge, the widows must begin to plead their case before the courts of heaven, and on earth, putting our righteous God in remembrance of His word. How much more will our Father in heaven hear us? The unrighteous judge declared "because this widow troubleth me, I will avenge her..."

Luke 18:7-8

7 And shall not God avenge his elect, which cry day and night unto him, though he bear long with them?

8 I tell you that he will avenge them speedily.

The widows must arise. Our voices are necessary for our deliverance. We cannot be afraid to "trouble" (parecho) our Father in heaven or the injustices in the earth. This greek word means to present oneself, hold near, and to cling to our Father and King until we have been avenged.

My prayer is that every widow will gain strength, power, and encouragement to recognize their right to accept, acknowledge, and identify with **THE WIDOWS MIGHT.**

1 ONLY GOD ESTABLISHES YOUR BORDERS

*THE **LORD** WILL DESTROY THE HOUSE OF THE PROUD, BUT HE WILL ESTABLISH THE BOUNDARY OF THE WIDOW.*

PROVERBS 15:25

The death of a spouse can make you feel helpless, hapless and hopeless. It is one of the most devastating events that can happen in a person's life. Per the Life Change Index Scale and several other studies, the death of a spouse is considered the most stressful life event that one encounters. This type of devastation impacts us psychologically and physically, even to the point that there is a **"widowhood effect"** which is the increase in the probability of a person dying in a relatively short time after their long-time spouse has died, generally within three months.

Obviously, with this level of vulnerability, shock, and devastation, the last thing that a widow feels are security, protection, and safety. The enemy of death has just snatched the most important person, the only one in life that can be counted as the same "one". So, the rush of emotions of widows/widowers is opposed to any sense of assurance, shelter or certainty. However, God steps into the situation of the widow and vows that He will establish her boundaries. The word establish is the Hebrew word natsab which means to fix, stand erect, to establish, and beset the boundary (territory, region) of the widow. So, God makes a vow that in this state of great confusion, havoc, and ruin, He will oversee the divine protection of the territory, assignment, and authority of the widow.

This promise is preceded by the acknowledgment that God will destroy the house of the proud, those who are arrogant, self-sufficient, and without reverence of His love and grace toward them. When our spouse has been taken from us, because of the covenant that God Himself established, that He is part of, He steps in.

"Therefore shall a man leave his father and his mother, and shall cleave unto his wife: and they shall be one flesh." Genesis 2:24

You see this covenant was God's idea. Becoming one flesh originated with Him. So, although the entrance of sin through disobedience was the actual source of the death and devastation of widowhood, in His loving-kindness and tender mercies, God retains His responsibility in the holy union that He alone established.

God made the man and the woman one flesh, and there is no other relationship other than husband and wife that was created to be intertwined, as one person. This is the only relationship that God says, "let no man put asunder." Thus, because of the covenant and declaration that God established in marriage, He also has made a commitment that when that covenant ends through death, that He will stand up and be your protection because He knows the depth of the tearing away of the only person on earth that He created for you to be as "one."

So, at the time when it feels like all is lost and life seems to make no sense, God then establishes the territory, authority, and boundaries (the marked and assigned place) of the widow. God lets us know in Isaiah 54 "thy maker is thy husband." So, just as a husband bands the house, God commits to protect, establish, define, identify and rise in the house of the widow.

I believe there is favor on the widow, that cannot come any other way. Why? Because in other situations like poverty, even orphans are not under a covenant that God ordained. Children are raised to leave their parents. "Therefore shall a man leave his father and mother." So, although these situations are also difficult, there is no equal to the impact to the soul as the death of a spouse that God proclaimed in Genesis 2:24, "and they shall be one flesh".

In the most tumultuous seasons of your life, God will establish, define and stretch you forth in territories, assignments and purpose that you would have never imagined. These are spaces and places that have been only reserved for the widow. Now is the time to look around and see how far-reaching and expanded your life purpose has become. Your territory has just been enlarged. It is not something you would have ever chosen; it has chosen you.

If you will open your eyes and ears and allow Holy Spirit to speak to you expressly, you will begin to see the higher calling, the expanded purpose, and what seems like destiny by a detour. But it is an established place that God has for you to be enlarged and to expand His Kingdom.

Do not allow anyone or anything to limit your dreams, expectations or aspirations. What you thought you could only accomplish with your spouse, may just be ordained for this season where God alone shows forth His favor towards you and establishes Himself as the ruler of your boundaries!

<u>PRAYER</u>

Father, I thank You that even in this place of devastation and transition, I will not limit myself or You. Establish the borders of my life, enlarge my territory in Jesus' name.

2 GOD EXECUTES JUSTICE ON YOUR BEHALF

"HE ADMINISTERS JUSTICE FOR THE
FATHERLESS AND THE WIDOW…"
DEUTERONOMY 10:18

Orphans, the poor, and widows are on the heart of God. He is concerned about the plight of the disadvantaged and the brokenhearted. Psalm 34:18 says that God is, "near to the brokenhearted." Know that God knows, understands and cares how the widow's heart has been torn apart and vows His divine protection concerning them.

Psalm 89:14 says that, "justice and judgment are the habitation of thy throne: mercy and truth shall go before thy face." The foundation of the throne of God is justice. Deuteronomy 10:18 translates that He becomes (administers) justice for the widow. God says to the widow I AM your justice. If God is for you, it is more than the world against you! In our most devastating hour, when it seems as if all is lost and that everything is falling apart, and that nothing will ever be as it was-----God steps in and becomes our justice, our authority, and our judicatory power!

How soothing and comforting to know that God Almighty vows to take a special and complete role on behalf of the hurting. Although we still must live through the pain, process it and properly place it, because it is real and a part of life and even the kingdom process, we have assured protection from our heavenly Father.

So, why are so many widows impoverished, mistreated, indigent, and ignored? How could this be? Well, Isaiah 1:17 (AMP) gives us a glimpse:

"Learn to do good; seek justice, rebuke the ruthless, defend the fatherless, plead for the [rights of the] widow [in court]."

Just like in the natural, justice does not generally come without a fight. The execution of justice is an indicator of injustice or inequities being in existence to require its administration. God has declared He becomes justice; however, we need to seek Him. To seek justice, we seek Him, true justice is never outside of Him. God said to seek justice and correct oppression. We all still have a role in ensuring that the cause of the widow is contended for but He guarantees that He will become justice, however, there is still a fight. Let every man be a liar, but let God be true!

The injustices that widows face being thrown into the street, having to fend for themselves and their children, not knowing where she may live or what her family may have to eat is a gross injustice. Particularly, when the widow supported a spouse that fought for their country, gave their lives to a community cause, lived a life of service, remained an upstanding citizen, contributed to the advancement of their community, and was a major factor in the success of their spouse. Justice is necessary but

justice must be sought. It doesn't come automatically. There must arise those who will contend for the widows.

PRAYER

Father, I thank You that I know that You become justice for widows, orphans, aliens and the poor. Holy Spirit teach me how to seek God, His mind and His justice concerning those who are hurting. I commit to know my assignment and role in aiding the widows, the poor, the orphans and the aliens.

3 GOD DEALS WITH YOUR OPPRESSORS

"CURSED IS HE WHO DISTORTS THE JUSTICE DUE AN ALIEN, ORPHAN, AND WIDOW."
DEUTERONOMY 27:19

I have found it comforting that in the place of my greatest vulnerability, God says that He will deal with my oppressors. We already know that vengeance belongs to God, but He takes it even further in regard to the intentional mistreatment and misrepresentation of those who are weak. In Exodus 22:22-24 God says, "You shall not afflict any widow or orphan. If you afflict him at all, and if he does cry out to Me, I will surely hear his cry; and My anger will be kindled, and I will kill you with the sword, and your wives shall become widows and your children fatherless."

Of course, we are under the dispensation of grace, and God's love and mercy prevail. However, God's eternal laws of the spirit are still in existence. Although it may not take on literal consequences, we will all reap what we sow. So, when we intentionally and wickedly mistreat those hurting, the harvest is multiplied. This type of injustice towards God's beloved will put the oppressor in the place of the same type of agony, having violated the law of the spirit toward those whom God Himself watches for their justice.

We must begin to become aware of the critical consequences of the violation of this spiritual law. Could this be one of the spiritual root causes of the decline in our communities, cities, and churches? In Deuteronomy 27, when the scripture speaks of "cursed is he who distorts the justice," the word distort is the Hebrew word natah, which means be gone, decline, and turn away from. So, there is a curse that comes from turning aside from the justice of the aliens, orphans, and widows. We cannot afford to ignore, decline, or pretend like we do not see, nor are aware of the gross suffering, inhumane treatment and even the discriminatory, prejudiced and inequitable laws and practices that plaque the aliens, orphans, and widows.

PRAYER

Father, I ask that You have mercy on those who have distorted justice towards the widows, whom You have vowed to protect. Help me to never ignore the alien, orphan, and widow. Open the eyes of Your people that we will never create the cause for a curse to be upon us.

4 GOD WILL TAKE AWAY YOUR REPROACH

*"FOR THOU... SHALT NOT REMEMBER THE REPROACH OF THY WIDOWHOOD ANY MORE." **ISAIAH 54:4***

There is a reproach that occurs in widowhood. Reproach is defined by the Oxford Advanced Learner Dictionary as, "a state of shame or loss of honor." This loss of honor reshapes the entire lives of widows, so that not only has her life been permanently altered by the departure of her soulmate, because many times, particularly in the case of a widow, the honor that she experienced as the wife of her spouse dissipates. It has been reported at life-loss.com that, "on average, widows lose around 75% of their social support network. Some people disappear immediately while others fade out of your life."

So, along with mourning their spouse, the life that now can never be, children they will never have, dreams that will not come to fruition, potential financial loss, and loss of identity as a couple, all add up to a complete transition of normalcy. Even what should be the circle of safety in close friends and family, many times begins to unravel.

In-laws sometimes become "outlaws." Children from previous marriages often rebel and distance themselves from the surviving spouse. Close "friends" who knew and identified with you as a couple many times will begin to disappear as they no longer can see the relationship without the significant other. There are a plethora of situations and circumstances that flip the world of a widow, and that brings a loss of honor, respect, recognition, and sometimes even trust.

The good news is that although God does not promise that this will not happen, He does promise you a glorious future that will cause you to not remember this reproach! How bright must be the future of the widow that trusts God, that He guarantees with the strongest language of the Bible, "Thou **shalt not** remember the reproach of thy widowhood."

No matter the situation, circumstance, loss, slander, betrayal, hurt, devastation, or abandonment, you have a future that God guarantees will bring such joy, faith, glory, and honor that you will forget the reproach you have suffered, and you will bask in the glory of His righteousness. Hallelujah!

<u>PRAYER</u>

Father, I thank You that despite my reproach I have hope and a future because You have said so. I thank You now because You are not a man that You should lie, neither the son of man that You should repent. So, I praise You now for the restoration of my soul, and Your glory and honor upon my life. In Jesus Name.

5 GOD COMMANDS YOUR PROVISION

"THE LORD ...RELIEVETH THE FATHERLESS AND WIDOW."
PSALMS 146:9

God declares that He is the support of the fatherless and widow. He even ties in blessings to those that bless the widow.

"When you reap your harvest in your field and have forgotten a sheaf in the field, you shall not go back to get it; it shall be for the alien, orphan, and the widow, so that the LORD your God may bless you in all the work of your hands." Deuteronomy 24:19

God commands the widows to be supported financially. He even goes further to attach a universal blessing upon the hands of those who remember the widow and do not just take everything for themselves.

God has made provisions for the weak, the problem has been that society has not heeded his command. We are to consider those less fortunate and calculate them in everything we do. Our laws, our ordinances, behaviors, and habits must begin to make provision for the aliens, orphans, and widows so that **ALL** the works of our hands will be blessed!

It is critical that on every level of society we begin to leave room for the less fortunate. Every segment of society can do its part to make provision. Starting with individuals, then families, communities, cities, and nations.

There is a blessing that comes when we care for the widows and alternatively, we are missing out on the fullness of God's blessings when we have neglected those He has commanded for us to provide for.

PRAYER

Father, we repent of neglecting those whom You have commanded us to provide for. Direct us to the alien, orphans or widows that You have ordained. We count it a privilege to extend Your heart and provision on Your behalf and we thank You in advance for the multiplied blessings that come when we obey You and care for those You have commanded.

6 GOD IS YOUR JUDGE

*"A FATHER OF THE FATHERLESS AND A JUDGE FOR THE WIDOWS, IS GOD IN HIS HOLY HABITATION." **PSALM 68:5***

No matter what your circumstances, remember that only God is your judge. Widowhood often brings guilt, condemnation, disgrace, regret, shame, and a host of many emotions. Unfortunately, sometimes the death of a spouse causes a widow to blame themselves, and unfortunately, sometimes others may also join the bandwagon.

The reality is that we are not even capable of judging others or ourselves. God is the only righteous judge and He is a judge of mercy, loving-kindness, and love. Whether you may be suffering from the regret of some things you may have done, or not done, it is important to not judge yourself. You are not equipped, nor do you possess the capacity to judge others or even your situation and life.

You mustn't allow any judgment to cloud your future by eliminating yourself from opportunities and occasions to expand, increase and multiply your life and your soul. You must know that God is a judge "for" you. He is not against you. Your entry into widowhood and your place in God's heart have new mercies daily distributed on your behalf. Do not allow past mistakes, regrets, and compunction to steer you to settle, alter, or minimize God's plan to bring you to an expected, expanded, and supernatural end.

PRAYER

Father, I thank You that You alone are my judge and You are a righteous judge. I repent of all sin and come boldly to the throne of grace to obtain mercy and help in this time of trouble. In all my ways, I acknowledge You and ask You to direct my path. Thank You for Your unfailing love and endless mercy towards me.

7 GOD IS YOUR PROTECTION

"I WILL BE QUICK TO TESTIFY AGAINST
SORCERERS, ADULTERERS, AND PERJURERS,
AGAINST THOSE WHO DEFRAUD LABORERS OF
THEIR WAGES, WHO OPPRESS THE WIDOWS AND
THE FATHERLESS, AND DEPRIVE THE
FOREIGNERS AMONG YOU OF JUSTICE."
MALACHI 3:5 NIV

One translation of Malachi 3:5 says that God will be a "swift" witness against those who oppress the widows. He will speedily and hurriedly defend, protect and be a testimony for His beloved. Are you in any way feeling or suffering from oppression? Put God in remembrance of His word. Call on Him to come quickly to your aid as a testimony and as a witness on your behalf. Because the weapons of our warfare are not carnal, but mighty through God in the pulling down of strongholds, you must remember that our oppression is not about people. The real enemy is the spirit that rules a people, a city, a culture, a nation.

Much of the suffering of the orphans, aliens, and widows are due to the ruling spirits that have been allowed to govern the hearts and minds of people. These spirits of lethargy, indifference, and insensitivity have caused our society to accept and be blinded by the sometimes harsh and inhumane conditions of many widows worldwide. Just as a witness is called to the stand as a testimony on behalf of the plaintiff, even though God has promised to be our witness, we still must call for Him! He told us to call on Him and He would answer us and show us great and mighty things that we don't even know.

God is waiting on us to call Him as our witness to be a testimony of glory, honor, and favor that we could have never known or even dreamed. Call on Him now!

<u>PRAYER</u>

Father in the Name of Jesus, You said that You would be a swift witness on my behalf. I know that You watch over Your word to perform it. Be my testimony now and cause my case to be final regarding Your love, purpose, honor, and favor upon my life.

8 GOD BECKONS FOR YOUR TRUST

"LET YOUR WIDOWS TRUST IN ME"
JEREMIAH 49:11

It is in our most challenging seasons that our faith and trust towards God are tested. It is when our lives are shattered and our future is bleak that God stretches out His hand towards us and beckons for us to trust Him. As a widow that has lost their soulmate, confidante, best friend, lover, and spouse, it is at that time that we are sorely reminded that "thy maker is thy husband," according to Isaiah 54.

Although God grants us the privilege of enjoying our lives with the one that He chose to walk by our sides, eventually the day comes where they are no longer there and God gently reminds us that all along it was He who gave us our spouses and they belong to Him. He then takes us on the journey of return to total reliance on Him. He graciously allowed us, during those times with our spouses, to attribute some of the comfort, reliance, and strength to them, when the source of all they provided was from Him.

So, as we experience widowhood, we are given a special invitation and opportunity to demonstrate our love, trust, and devotion to our maker.

1 Timothy 5:5 says, "Now she that is a widow indeed, and desolate, trusteth in God, and continueth in supplications and prayers night and day." God wants us to trust Him even when we don't understand Him. He is beckoning you now to trust what He has allowed.

PRAYER

Father, I repent of all fear, doubt, unbelief and my tendency not to trust You and what You have allowed to transpire in my life. I recognize now that even in this I must trust that You will work all things together for my good, that You are with me and will never forsake me, and that Your thoughts of me are thoughts of good and not evil to bring me to an expected end. Into Your hands, I commit my spirit and I command my soul to, "trust in God!"

9 YOU ARE DUE HONOR

"HONOR WIDOWS WHO ARE WIDOWS INDEED."
1 TIMOTHY 5:3

We have specific instructions to honor or "timao" widows, which means revere, value, and venerate them. High value is to be affixed to widows. Although, in context to the scriptures Paul goes on to define, "widows indeed" as those who have no family, children, or nephews to care for them. The scriptures also separate the younger widows from the older ones, as Paul acknowledges that the younger widows may be more susceptible to physical desires.

Regardless of age, honor, and care are still necessary. Some of our laws regarding widows reflect the opposite of Paul's instruction. Widows with small children receive ample care and assistance, while older women under 60 regardless of if they have children or not, will not be able to receive social security until they reach the age of 60.

Overall, the essence or spirit of the scriptures instruct the families, and all involved to properly care for their widows, and for widows to live an honorable life. Particularly widows who served their husbands, brought up their children, took in strangers, relieved the afflicted and practiced good works--- we have a responsibility, the families, churches, and the community----to honor and care for the widows.

With this being the case how can so many churches with widows not be in tune with the plight of the widow? Even worse, the pattern of expunging the widow of the pastor, bishop or apostle immediately upon the death of the leader. There have been several stories in recent headlines where widows that served in major movements alongside their husbands for decades were cast out, disregarded and disrespected after serving and giving their entire lives faithfully to their spouses, children, ministry, and communities. This should not be named among the redeemed!

"But if any provide not for his own, and especially for those of his own house, he hath denied the faith, and is worse than an infidel." (1 Timothy 5:8)

Many times, this scripture is quoted about a man taking care of his house. This is not the context of this scripture. The context of this scripture is amid the narrative about the widow! As verse 9 continues: "Let not a widow be taken into the number under threescore years old, having been the wife of one man."

This scripture was in direct reference to the care of widows. May God have mercy on the churches, ministries, organizations, families, and individuals that refuse to provide for their own while they pretend to be in the faith. God says they are worse than an infidel (apistos), heathen, unbeliever, faithless and untrustworthy!

PRAYER

Father, I pray that You will open our eyes to honor all those that You have commanded us to honor as we know that true honor requires substance and not mere words. Thank You that I am to be honored and I shall give honor where it is due. Open the eyes of Your people and open our ears to hear what Your Spirit is saying to the church. Bless all Your widows and may we live lives that bring honor to You and Your Kingdom in Jesus' Name.

10 YOU ARE SOMEBODY'S ANSWER

"A BROTHER IS BORN FOR ADVERSITY"
PROVERBS 17:17

Everything that you have gone through God uses to strengthen and settle you. Our suffering is part of the process of building us and preparing for us to reign. As hard as it is to accept, even this, the loss of the love of your life, can and will be used to bring glory to God, to strengthen you and to build you up so that you can be a shelter and help for others.

Romans 5:3-4 tells us the process and purpose of our tribulations. In every tribulation, we are growing in our faith and character which produces the fruit of the Spirit. Our tribulation produces patience, patience produces experience, and experience produces hope, which is the main ingredient in our faith.

31

So, our hurt and pain eventually leads us to a hope that is sure and unmovable. As God navigates us through the most traumatic part of our lives, He establishes His faithfulness and it produces hope and trust that there is no circumstance that with God we cannot prevail.

As you enter this realm in the Spirit of God, you now become an answer for someone else. Having now become "converted" you can strengthen your brother. God uses our testimonies to strengthen our brothers and to cause them to overcome.

"And they overcame him by the blood of the Lamb, and by the word of their testimony" Revelation 12:11

Authentic hope is not present until we have produced it through the context of suffering, not in the expectation of pleasure! This is the hope that we have, that anchors our souls and makes our souls firm and secure. The hope that was formed through some of the greatest trials of our lives. You and your adversity become the answer or the hope for others to overcome. Do not ever give up, because somebody is waiting for their answer!

PRAYER

Father, I thank You that I know that You are raising me to be an answer to someone's adversity. I know that in my weakness Your strength is made perfect, so I thank You for perfect strength to be my portion so that I can endure, develop the patience, experience and hope that You have ordained for me to carry so that I may be an answer to those to whom You have assigned me. Thank You, Lord that I am the answer!

11 THE TALE OF THREE WIDOWS

*"AND ORPAH KISSED HER MOTHER IN LAW:
BUT RUTH CLAVE
UNTO HER." **RUTH 1:14***

One of the most powerfully significant stories of the strength, authority, favor, and demonstration of God's promises to the widow can be found in the book of Ruth.

We find this powerful story of one matriarch, Naomi, whose husband dies while dwelling in Moab, a place where their family came because of a great famine. Can you imagine having been forced to live in a foreign place and while there, your husband dies? It is hard enough to lose a spouse in a familiar place, surrounded by friends and family. But Naomi had to endure the loss of her spouse in a foreign land, and was left with her two sons.

Soon, her two sons married Moabite women, Ruth and Orpah. However, within 10 years, both of Naomi's sons died as well. So now, these three widows were left to fend for themselves and create a new life.

Ruth 1:6-7

6 Then she arose with her daughters in law, that she might return from the country of Moab: for she had heard in the country of Moab how that the LORD had visited his people in giving them bread.

7 Wherefore she went forth out of the place where she was, and her two daughters in law with her; and they went on the way to return unto the land of Judah.

Naomi and her family had originally come to Moab to escape the family. Now, after having lost everything, Naomi received word that there was a blessing among her people in her native land.

I have discovered that for many widows, what was left, abandoned, and possibly what you walked away from in your old season, will become illuminated, reactivated and brought back to life in your new season. It may have been a career, a skill, a desire to travel or a hobby that you put down in order to serve your spouse, raise your kids, or simply live the life that you created for a specific time. However, do not be surprised if you begin to "hear" the call of your native core giftings, talents and desires begin to be reactivated during your new season of widowhood.

As Naomi headed back to the place of blessing, she gave her two daughters in law the opportunity to go back to their homes. Orpah kissed her mother in law, said goodbye and headed home. However, Ruth cleaved to Naomi and later became a blessing to her mother in law who was her mentor and teacher.

The tale of these three widows represent a powerful model of recovery during this season of grieving. You can either go back to the familiar, like Orpah. Or you can proceed to the blessed place, like Naomi and Ruth. What is familiar is not always the blessed place, and the blessed place is not always familiar!

The dynamics of Naomi and Ruth are also of note as I believe that in your season of recovery you should become both Naomi and Ruth. As Naomi, you commit to pouring into others, using your experience and wisdom to impart and to impact those that need your specific expertise and input. Proverbs 11:25 says "he that watereth shall be watered also himself."

One of the keys to recovering is in the refreshing waters that come as a result of selflessly pouring into others even in the midst of one of the worst times of your life.

However, to only pour in this season of recovering could be dangerous mentally, spiritually, and emotionally. So, it is important to also become Ruth in this season, and find a mentor, coach, or spiritual parent to pour into you, provide counsel, insight, deliverance or therapy, so that you can become whole while actively engaging in relationships, which are the key to our mental, social, and emotional development.

The healthiest emotional development requires that we have relationships that include each dimension of interaction, mentors, friends, and mentees. By maintaining relationships on each of these levels, we continue to develop skill sets, interactive capacity, and relationship acumen while still in recovery and expansion of our new life and renewed possibilities.

The journey for Naomi was not an easy one, as none of this is easy for any of us. Upon returning to her homeland she did not want to be called by her name, Naomi, which means "my pleasant one." She asked that they call her "Mara: for the Almighty hath dealt very bitterly with me." Ruth 1:20

In the midst of so much loss, many widows lose more than a spouse, they may lose friendships, social status, their home, and so much more. The enemy would want you to become bitter, when God has declared your life to be a pleasant one, an abundant life, from the beginning of time. Do not allow the events of your life to usurp God's declaration for you.

I've seen a pattern that much like Naomi, there is generally more than one tragedy that may be in close proximity to the loss of your spouse. Recently, a well-known minister lost his wife to cancer, with just a month before, he was mourning his father's death.

My husband died on January 16th, then my children's grandmother on their father's side passed away on February 16th. My mother then also transitioned on April 1st. As my husband's death was unexpected and a great shock to me, I remained numb throughout the deaths that followed, even my own mothers'. Add to that the pressures of taking on all of the organizations that my husband left to my care, dealing with the day to day operations of them, as well as the transitional fall out and relational adjustments that occur when a spouse dies. Nothing is the same. People do not treat you the same, or even see you the same, even sometimes those whom you trusted the most.

We can all relate to how Naomi felt. But, we must not succumb to the temptation to feel sorry for ourselves or to every speak from our mouths anything other than what God has said concerning our lives. Naomi went on to be a teacher and mentor for Ruth. Through Naomi's favor, wisdom, and experience, Ruth gained the favor of Boaz, a man of wealth in the lineage of Naomi. The union of Ruth and Boaz became a blessing to both Naomi and Ruth as Obed was birthed from this union, the father of Jesse, the father of David, part of the lineage of our Lord and Savior Jesus Christ!

This story reverberates many of the principles we have discussed regarding the favor of God upon widows. When Naomi returned to her place of promise, she had the favor of God. As Ruth gleaned in the field and helped to take care of her mother in law, she had the favor and protection of God and man. When Ruth, a Moabite, joined in marriage with Boaz, she received a covenant blessing upon her life, a blessing that should not have been given to a foreigner. However, God blessed these widows to defy laws and historical practices.

Ruth 4:11-12

11 And all the people that were in the gate, and the elders, said, we are witnesses. The LORD make the woman that is come into thine house like Rachel and like Leah, which two did build the house of Israel: and do thou worthily in Ephratah, and be famous in Bethlehem:

12 And let thy house be like the house of Pharez, whom Tamar bare unto Judah, of the seed which the LORD shall give thee of this young woman.

The significance of a woman who had a pagan heritage to be given a covenant blessing, likened to the matriarchs of the house of Israel, Leah and Rachel translates to a supernatural establishment of the boundaries that only God Himself will set on your behalf.

As you continue to walk in gratefulness, humility and honor, God will make you into a great nation. He will make your name great, establish your borders, bless you, and see to it that all of the families of the earth are blessed through you and your seed!

Naomi ultimately was blessed and restored out of her "bitter" season, because she traveled to the blessed place, and she poured into another vessel. Ruth received her blessing because she honored and followed her ordained mentor, obeyed her, and selflessly upheld the God and the guidelines of her ordained mentor, in the midst of her mourning and establishing her new normal.

Ruth gave birth to a son, another extension of her boundary, as she had not borne children before. Could it be that this is the season that what you were not able to give birth to in your last season, God has ordained for you new season? Don't be surprised that you will birth what you could not birth before. God has a special time and place for your "Obed" (life of service) to be birthed. He has assigned people, places and things in this season of your life to restore, renew, and revive you once again!

Ruth 4:15

And he shall be unto thee a restorer of thy life, and a nourisher of thine old age: for thy daughter in law, which loveth thee, which is better to thee than seven sons, hath born him.

PRAYER

Father, I thank You that I shall hear Your call to the place of blessing. Thank You for directing me specifically to my purpose and destiny for this season and this hour. I thank You for surrounding me with those that will be a blessing, and that I too will bless. I thank You that I know my times are in Your hands and that You shall bring me to an expected end, one of good and not of evil, surrounded by Your favor, grace and glory. In Jesus' Name.

CONCLUSION

54 SO WHEN THIS CORRUPTIBLE SHALL HAVE PUT ON INCORRUPTION, AND THIS MORTAL SHALL HAVE PUT ON IMMORTALITY, THEN SHALL BE BROUGHT TO PASS THE SAYING THAT IS WRITTEN, DEATH IS SWALLOWED UP IN VICTORY.55 O DEATH, WHERE IS THY STING? O GRAVE, WHERE IS THY VICTORY? 57 BUT THANKS BE TO GOD, WHICH GIVETH US THE VICTORY THROUGH OUR LORD JESUS CHRIST.

1 CORINTHIANS 15:54-55, 57

God promises victory over death. The paradoxical nature of the Kingdom resounds in the fact that we actually pass from life to "life" through the channel of death. So, as the enemy of death grabs hold of our victorious state of the incorruptible and eternal victory that Jesus Christ died for!

It is our faith in this sure and complete promise of God, that enables us to continue to declare the victory even through our pain.

I want to mention that because this book is biblically based, the widower, although not often mentioned, is not excluded from our love, care and concern. Although the scriptures do not address the widower as it does the widow, it is our responsibility to "mourn with those who mourn" and to "comfort those with the same comfort of which we have been comforted". The widower also needs support, prayers, love and grace extended. Whether widow or widower, the promises of God remain yes and amen!

It is great to know that this victory over death is not a promise just to the widows/widowers. It is a promise to every believer. We have victory over natural and spiritual death, through the blood of Jesus and His promises of resurrected life. We can overcome the death of our dreams, visions, hope, and yes even the death of our loved ones, as His love, grace and mercy extends to our hearts and souls to bring forth healing and restoration.

Although we will always remember our loved ones and will continue to carry a remnant of pain from that loss, the victory through Christ Jesus is never lost, and His grace remains eternally sufficient to see us through every twist and turn that life sends us all through. As the Bible says in Psalms 68:20 "unto GOD the Lord belong the issues from death." It is God alone through which we can "escape" death. We can escape its reproach, grief, fear, and sting. As we continue to trust what our Father has allowed, grab hold of His peace that surpasses all understanding, and declare all of the promises that He has given to us during this season in our lives, we will begin to behold the beauty of His holiness and the fragrance of His presence. Whatever your situation, continue to put God in remembrance of His promises, do not relent, because He will give you justice!

PRAYER

Father, I thank You that I know that death has no victory because of the blood of Jesus my Lord and Savior. I thank You that I know that my loved one has passed from life to life, because to be absent from the body is to be present with You. I take comfort in this knowledge of the eternal life that awaits us all that believe and trust in You. I commit all things concerning life and death unto You, and I call for Jehovah Shalom to dwell with me as I receive Your peace that does not require me to understand. Thank You Father for all of the promises You have made to the widows, I shall forget them not, and I put You in remembrance of every benefit that You have declared concerning me. I know that You are not a man that you should lie, neither the son of man that You should repent, so I come boldly before Your throne to receive the blessings that You load me with today and forever more, in Jesus' Name, amen.

PRAYER OF SALVATION

If you have not accepted Jesus Christ as Lord and Savior, this is your opportunity to receive His love, mercy, and grace that will not only lead to a more abundant life on earth, but also will prepare the way for you to live eternally in heaven with him forever more.

Psalm 91:14-16

Because he has set his love on me, therefore will I deliver him: I will set him on high, because he has known my name. He shall call on me, and I will answer him: I will be with him in trouble; I will deliver him, and honor him. With long life will I satisfy him, and show him my salvation.

If you desire to experience the greatest love of all, repeat this prayer in faith, and call on the one and only true and living God and you will experience the power of salvation through Jesus Christ.

PRAYER

Father, I confess my sin and I turn away from all unrighteousness, as I now confess Jesus as my Lord and Savior. Your word declares that every one that calls upon the name of the Lord shall be saved. As I call upon You and have confessed Jesus as Lord, and I believe that by Your Spirit You raised Him from the dead so that I may have everlasting life, I receive the gift of salvation now, in the name of Jesus Christ my Lord.

EPILOGUE

It is my hope that this book will create the dialogue needed to help change the mental, emotional, social and financial plight of the widow. According to the Social Security Administration "women have higher poverty rates in old age than men, in large part because they earn less over a lifetime and live longer. Greater longevity also means that many women will spend some time during their life course as widows. Estimates from the Current Population Survey show that the poverty rate for women aged 65 or older in 2008 was almost double (11.9 percent) that of men (6.7 percent)."

With these staggering statistics coupled with the fact that Social Security remains the only major source of assistance for widows, there is a need to review and revise our legislation, social security, and our social responsibility as families, communities, churches, and as a nation. We cannot afford to continue to ignore the plight of the widow. One of the most difficult life events that anyone could face, should be met with a level of support, humanity and sensitivity to the basic rights and needs of productive citizens. I encourage you to contact your local.

senator, church, or business to become involved in the efforts to care for the orphan, foreigner, poor and the widow.

ABOUT THE AUTHOR

Apostle Darlyn C. Turner has a vast arsenal of skills, abilities, and gifting. As a producer, minister, coach, author, and leader of several organizations, including Billionaire Minds, a nonprofit organization dedicated to training and cultivating entrepreneurial skills and vision. Darlyn recently founded The National Widows Association, a 501c3 organization dedicated to the advancement and empowerment of widows.

Darlyn is also the President of Holywood Studios, a Christian film and production company started by her late husband, Dr. Clifford E. Turner, the writer, producer, and director of the Emmy Award Winning series, The Awakening. She is the co-producer of the Women on the Move series, a nationally syndicated television series. Also, after the death of her husband, Darlyn became the President of The Liberty International Network, a collaborative of ministries, churches, businesses, and individuals dedicated to the advancement of the kingdom of God extending to all sectors of society. As a former executive of a Fortune 500 company, Darlyn has combined her experience, training, and skills to serve her community, mentor, and aid in the development of future leaders.

Apostle Darlyn's ultimate call and passion is to women and their empowerment. She has hosted several national women's conferences for over 20 years, and is a mentor to many women, helping them to fully embrace their identity, power, and purpose to fulfill their destinies and thrive mentally, physically, financially, and spiritually.

Apostle Darlyn's coaching, ministry, and expertise, which are timeless and genderless, transcend culture and lead to inner healing, personal empowerment, and success in life by opening both minds and hearts. Darlyn has made her mark in the municipalities, the marketplace and in ministry.

Darlyn resides in both the Chicagoland and Orlando areas. She currently has nine children and 4 grandchildren.

For more information about Apostle Darlyn you can visit her website at darlynturner.com

CONTACT THE AUTHOR

Website: thenwaonline.com

Email: nwaonline@yahoo.com

Address: 378 Commons Drive,
Bolingbrook, IL 60440

If you desire to help The National Widows Association get this book in the hands of every widow possible, and consider donating at thenwaonline.com

Made in the USA
Columbia, SC
27 June 2024

37529029R00037